To

From

WHY YOU'RE MY BEST FRIEND

My Best Friend

I wrote this book for you as a way of showing my love and appreciation. I am the person I am today thanks to your friendship and support.

This book contains some treasured memories of our friendship, and it is an expression of my gratitude to you for being the greatest friend I could ever ask for.

1

I CHERISH OUR BOND BECAUSE...

2

WE HAVE THE MOST FUN WHEN WE...

3

THERE IS NO ONE LIKE YOU, WHO CAN...

4

YOU BRING OUT THE BEST IN ME BY...

5

I ADMIT THAT YOU'LL ALWAYS BE BETTER THAN I AM AT...

6

EVEN WHEN YOU DON'T WANT TO, YOU ALWAYS...

7

I WILL NEVER GET BORED WITH YOUR...

8

THE MOST IMPORTANT THING YOU EVER DID FOR ME WAS...

SOME OF MY FAVORITE SAYINGS OF YOURS ARE...

9

WE MAKE THE BEST TEAM AT...

10

YOU CAN CHEER ME UP JUST BY...

11

MY FAVORITE DAYS TOGETHER ARE WHEN WE...

12

I'D LOVE IT IF ONCE AGAIN WE COULD...

13

YOU SOMEHOW KNOW JUST WHAT (OR WHAT NOT!) TO SAY WHEN...

14

PEOPLE BETTER WATCH OUT IF THEY MESS WITH YOUR...

15

YOU DEFINITELY WIN THE AWARD FOR...

SOME
OF MY
FAVORITE
NICKNAMES
FOR YOU
ARE...

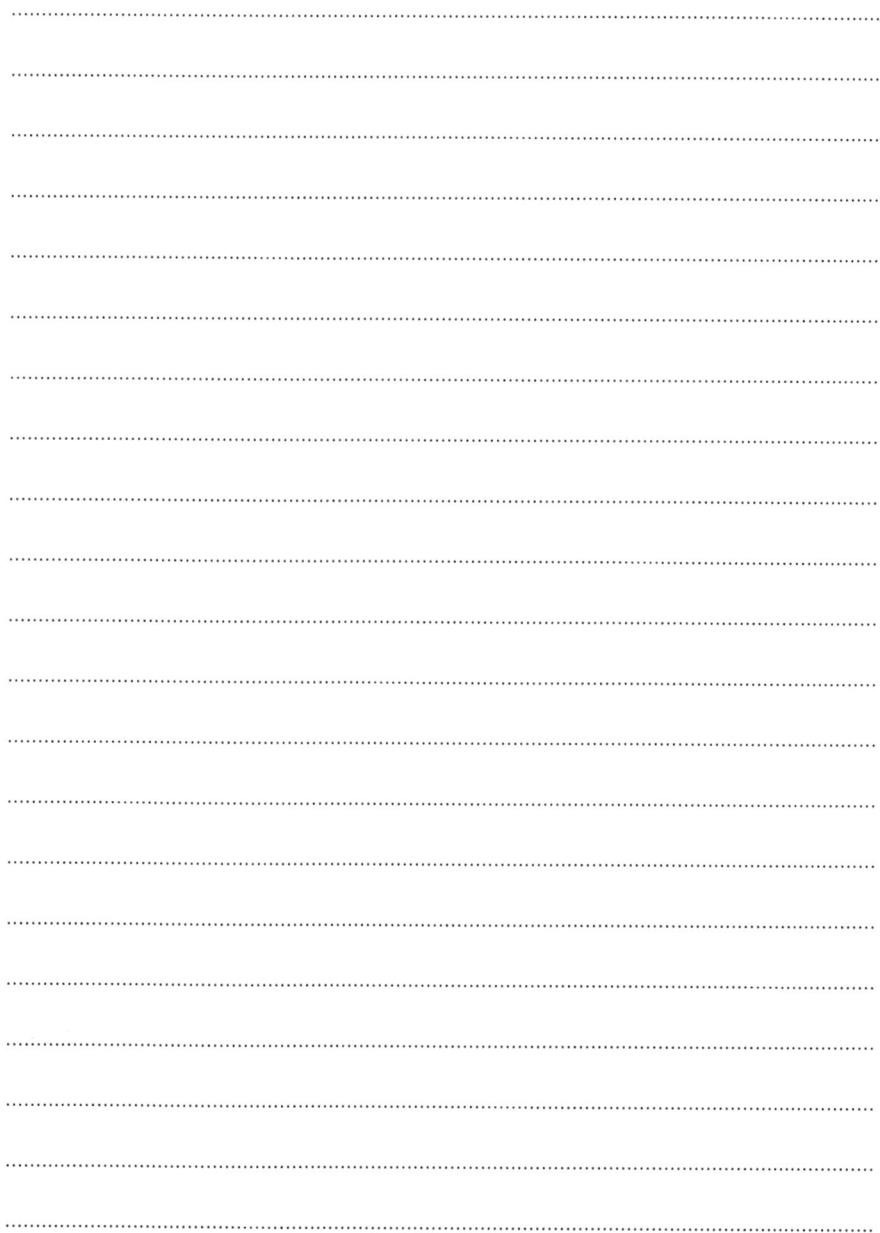

16

YOU ALWAYS GIVE THE BEST ADVICE ABOUT...

17

I LOVE THAT YOU DON'T CARE ABOUT...

18

YOU ALWAYS ENCOURAGE ME TO...

19

WHEN WE ARE TOGETHER, WE ALWAYS...

20

YOUR GREATEST SUPERPOWER IS...

21

I LOVE HOW WE CAN JOKE ABOUT...

22

YOU HAVE A WAY OF MAKING PEOPLE FEEL...

SOME OF THE MOST MEMORABLE MOMENTS WE'VE SHARED ARE...

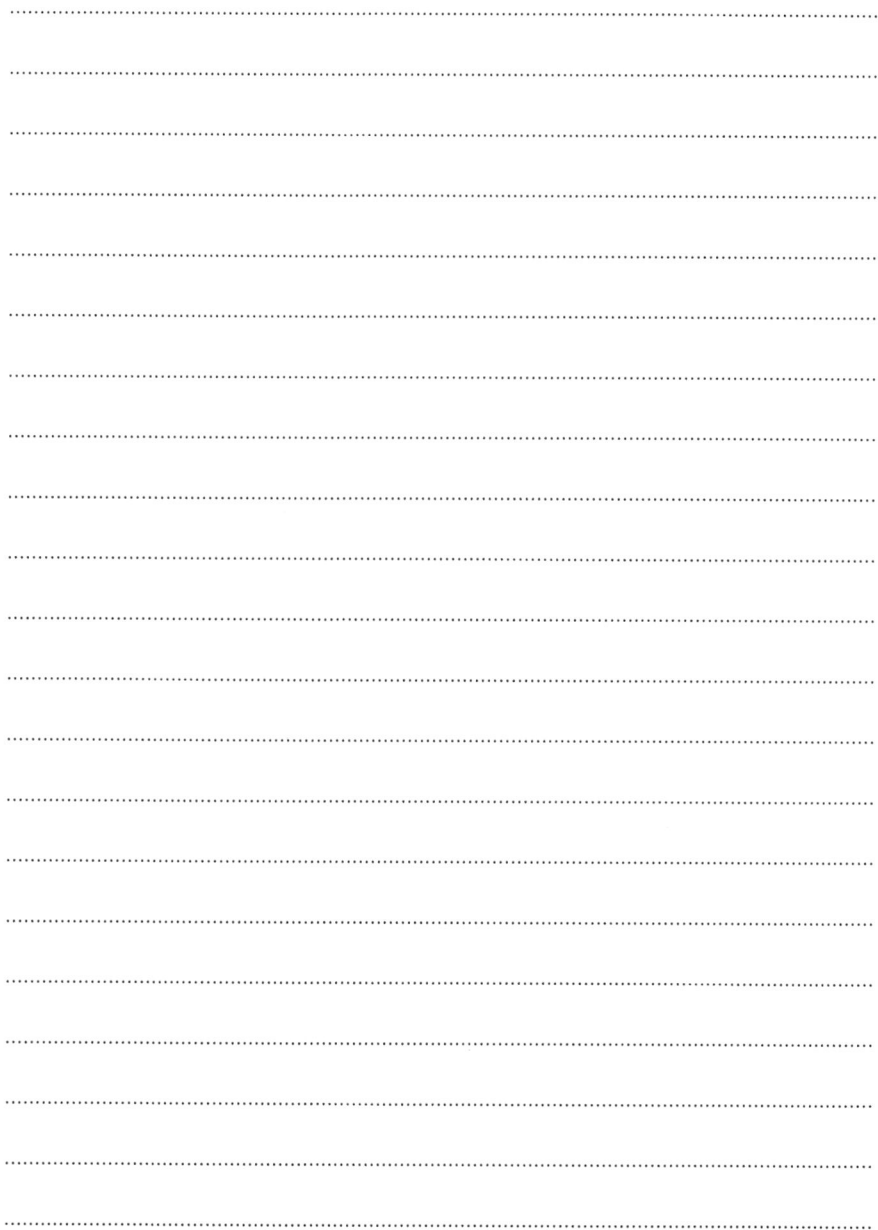

23

IF YOU WERE AN EMOJI, YOU'D BE...

24

THANK YOU FOR ALWAYS BEING HONEST ABOUT...

25

YOU HAVE THE BEST TASTE WHEN IT COMES TO...

26

IF WE COULD GO ANYWHERE IN THE WORLD TOGETHER, WE WOULD GO...

27

YOU ALWAYS MAKE ME LAUGH WHEN YOU...

28

THANK YOU FOR ALWAYS...

29

I'D BE LOST WITHOUT YOUR...

30

YOU'RE A GREAT FRIEND BECAUSE...

YOU'RE MY
BEST
FRIEND

Why You're My Best Friend by Questions About Me™

www.questionsaboutme.com

IMPORTANT INSTRUCTIONS

Before completing this book, please read our important **How-To Guide.**

Inside the How-To Guide you'll find:

- Suggested ideas for each prompt in the book
- Hints and tips on completing the book

To access the How-To Guide, simply scan the QR code below

Or visit
www.questionsaboutme.com/bestie